TICKETS NOT TRANSFERABLE
The Photo Album of a Tyneside Train Spotter

Les Turnbull

**ERGO
PRESS**
Publishing for Northumberland

TICKETS NOT TRANSFERABLE
The Photo Album of a Tyneside Train Spotter
2nd Edition (revised) January 2008

First published by
ERGO PRESS
©Les Turnbull 2007

ISBN: 0-9552758-6-5
ISBN: 978-0-9552758-6-9

ERGO
PRESS
5, St Mary's Chare
Hexham
Northumberland
NE46 1NQ

ergo.press@yahoo.co.uk
www.ergopress.com
01434 689653
Written and published in Northumberland

Contents

The author, aged fourteen, on the footplate of Class B16/1 61413
at Heaton South Yard one Sunday in August 1956.
The photograph was taken by his father, who was on duty at the time.

To my grand daughters
Katherine and Yasmin,
train-spotters of the future.

Foreword

As one of the original members of the Redhill Gang, it is an honour to be asked to write the foreword to 'Tickets Not Transferable' (I am the lanky one on the extreme right in the photograph). Having had, like Les, a lifetime's interest in railways, one outcome has been to visit places not normally on tourist itineraries, both in the United Kingdom and world wide. From Vladivostok (yes, we train-spotters have travelled the Trans-Siberian Railway), Murmansk and Pechenga to Consett, Dowlais Central, Tondu, Tallington, Lyme Regis and Hayling Island, we have explored the railway systems of the world.

Train-spotting is often thought of as serving no useful purpose – but how wrong this assessment can be. In my case, seeing ex North British Railway 'Scotts' and ex London and North Eastern Railway 'Scottish Directors' gave a curious schoolboy an everlasting love of reading Sir Walter Scott's 'Waverley' novels. Engine names such as 'Dugald Dalgetty', 'Wandering Willie' and 'Laird of Balmawhapple' had to be traced to their origins. Modern locomotive names do not have the same magic.

All of the members of the Redhill Gang did extremely well in their various careers and many led distinguished professional lives in banking, education, the sciences and engineering. Today, members of the gang are scattered throughout the world but they still retain the love of rail travel which was so instrumental in broadening their intellects during their formative years.

May this book serve as a tribute to our band of brothers – the Redhill Gang.

Dr -Ing Professor Frederick William Hampson
Newcastle upon Tyne, February 2007

About the Author

After his train-spotting teens, Les Turnbull was awarded a BA (Hons) from Durham University. He taught in the North East and in Canada before becoming a lecturer in the Education Department of the University of Newcastle upon Tyne. He later became Senior Education Advisor for Gateshead MBC before retiring and becoming a full time grandfather and author. His earlier work, The History of Lead Mining in the North East of England was published in 2006.

A FAMILY TRADITION

The world has changed enormously since these photographs were taken in the mid 1950s. They illustrate a world that has been lost, both in the sense that features of it no longer exist, as in the case of the vanished station at Rothbury (below), and in the sense that aspects of it have changed beyond recognition, like Newcastle Central Station where some of the platforms have been replaced by car parks. Above all, the

Class J21 65110 (52B), Rothbury, 13 April 1957

steam locomotive has disappeared from the everyday life of the region; the dirt, the smoke and the smell of oil and steam no longer pervade the atmosphere. The scream of the engine's whistle and the clanking of wagons being shunted are sounds of the past.

The album also illustrates a popular hobby of the time – train-spotting. The number of railway enthusiasts has fallen dramatically with the demise of the steam locomotive and crowds of adolescent boys no longer huddle with their notebooks at the end of station platforms. Although new steam locomotives were still being built in the mid 1950s, many train-spotters were conscious that the age of steam would eventually disappear and they tried to make a photographic record of it before it was too late. However, it never crossed our minds that there was only a decade left. Not only were branch line services axed – such as the train from Manors to Newbiggin-by-the-Sea seen leaving Newsham (below) – but also stations on the main line such as Annitsford were closed and even entire railways including the branch to Middleton-in-Teesdale disappeared.

Class V1 67651 (52B), Newsham, January 1957

Class D20/1 62396 (52D), approaching Annitsford, September 1957

This is a very personal account, because I took all of the photographs myself, and the collection is arranged to show what we railway enthusiasts did in the mid 1950s. It illustrates not only the bygone railways but also a lost teenage hobby belonging to a less materialistic and more innocent age. Fifty years ago the life of a teenager was very different from that of today's adolescents. For most of the youngsters growing up in the east end of Newcastle there were no televisions, no computers and the only telephone was a public one in a red box at the corner of the street. There were very few cars. Consequently, football games could be played in the streets of terraced houses, an activity which is impossible in the same streets today because of the volume of traffic. Football was one popular pastime for boys and another absorbing passion was the railway.

Class L1 67705 (32B), Cotherstone, 26 May 1958
Running in after a visit to Darlington North Road workshops.

The main east coast railway line linking Newcastle with Edinburgh carved its way in a semi-circle through Heaton. The photograph below shows an Edinburgh express passing through Heaton Junction.

Class A2 60534 'Irish Elegance' (64B)
Heaton Junction, August 1956

Day and night, we could hear the thunderous clatter of express trains or the ponderous straining of heavy freight locomotives. There were three marshalling yards at the bottom of our street, and the shunting of wagons was an ever-present background noise. There were also a large locomotive depot housing over one hundred steam engines, carriage sidings and workshops for building wagons.

The photograph overleaf shows a heavy freight train struggling north up Benton Bank from Heaton New Yard.

Class V2 60947 (52A), climbing Benton Bank, August 1956

Many people living in the terraces worked on the railway, including my father, who was one of the inspectors in the marshalling yards. Because of this, the rhythm of our household was governed by the shifts of the railway. Night shift (10pm to 6am) meant that my father had to sleep during the day; this was not a problem during school term, but in the holidays it was wise to keep out of the way. Early shift (6am to 2pm) was great, because Dad was at home when we returned from school. On back shift (2pm to 10pm) I often had to take my father's bait down to the inspector's cabin after school; this provided an opportunity to get near to the locomotives and sometimes (what joy!) to spend an evening in the signal cabin.

Lighting-up time at Heaton Shed
Class D49/2 62744 'The Holderness' (62B), Heaton, September 1956

The railway even affected the very atmosphere in which we lived. You could smell the fish-train pass and everyone knew when the bone train was in Heaton sidings! The photograph on the previous page shows 'lighting-up time' at Heaton Shed, when the fires in the engines were lit. In the autumn it was quite often impossible to see across the road because of the smog to which the railway made a major contribution. All of this inconvenience was accepted as part of everyday life.

One of the great advantages of having a parent who worked on the railway was having access to free passes and privilege tickets; these enabled me to explore the railways throughout Britain very cheaply. Reproduced above is an application form for a privilege ticket which was taken to the booking clerk (in this case at Hexham) to purchase a privilege ticket or 'P.T.'. An example of such a ticket for the journey from Newcastle to Hawick is reproduced on the previous page; it so happens that it was for the last train (see *Lost Routes*). More precious were the free passes, which were limited in number depending upon the grade of the employee. Three passes are reproduced on this page, issued to 'Master L. Turnbull' in 1957.

My Grandfather
Bob Gordon

My Father
Les Turnbull

My mother worked in the booking office at Newcastle Central Station. My grandfather, Bob Gordon, also worked on the railway, although in a much more prestigious position: he was a top link driver at Heaton Shed in charge of the main line expresses, including the royal train. The Gordons lived in the houses built by the North Eastern Railway in Spencer Street, next to the marshalling yards and engine shed. The photograph shows my father in his uniform, outside the inspector's cabin at Heaton North Yard. The piercing eyes of a first class locoman are evident in my grandfather's portrait. My uncle, Stephen Webb, was also a top link driver at Heaton. In the

My uncle Stephen Webb with Class A3 'St Gatien' at Heaton Shed

photograph he is dwarfed by the 6'8" driving wheels of his favourite engine at Heaton Shed, the Gresley A3 Pacific 'St Gatien'. Given this background it is really not surprising that I became a railway enthusiast.

Caledonian Class 3F 56275 (65F), Grangemouth, August 1956

This book is autobiographical but the experiences described were typical of those of teenagers across the country who followed the absorbing hobby of train-spotting. The photograph above shows Tyneside train-spotters in action, bunking the engine shed at Grangemouth. 'Bunking' was a term used throughout the country for visiting a shed without permission – trespassing. Unlike today, in the mid 1950s railways in different areas of the country had their own distinctive features, reflecting the identities of the four major companies which had been amalgamated to form British Railways in 1948. To observe all of this, railway enthusiasts travelled widely to visit engine sheds, railway centres and humble branch lines. However, they all started on their own home patch ...

OUR HOME PATCH

Throughout the country, railway enthusists of all ages gathered at the end of the platform or some other vantage point along the line to watch the trains, like the youngsters below at Bala Station in North Wales.

GWR 0-6-0 Pannier Tank 8791 (84F), Bala

I was a member of the Redhill Gang which met most evenings opposite Little Benton South signal cabin, on land which is now next to Newcastle United Football Academy. On Saturdays, we would take the Alnwick train (below) from Killingworth or Forest Hall to Newcastle Central for a day's train-spotting. Our 'home patch' was the stretch of line from the Central to Killingworth, which the photographs in this chapter illustrate.

Class D20/1 62395 (52D), Little Benton South, 7 September 1957

Newcastle Central Station was a great railway centre in the age of steam, handling about fifteen million passengers each year. There was also an abundance of freight traffic passing on the four tracks behind the station. On the next page is the west end of the station, where the train for Carlisle leaves beneath a large gantry of semaphore signals. Unlike today, it will travel on the north side of the river, past the Forth Goods Depot, where a freight train lurks in the gloom.

Class B1 61065 (50B), Newcastle Central, September 1956

In the image below, the 'station pilot', no longer a feature of the railway, shunts a set of coaches. These were fussy little engines, constantly moving stock around to assemble trains.

Class J72 68720 (52A), Newcastle Central, November 1956

In the 1950s freight traffic was the principal source of revenue for the railways and, unlike today, there was a constant flow of goods traffic passing behind the station.

The picture opposite (above) shows a local freight engine in shabby condition heading for the Forth Goods Depot. Opposite (below) a tank engine arrives with empty stock from Heaton carriage sidings. A grimy streamlined A4 'Silver King' from Gateshead depot waits to depart with an express for London King's Cross, (p.18). These streamlined engines were affectionately known as 'Streaks' because they hauled the fastest express trains of the day, streaking along the east coast main line (see p.38).

Class J25 65675 (52B), Newcastle Central, September 1956

Class V1 67641 (52B), Newcastle Central, August 1956

Class A4 60016 'Silver King' (52A), Newcastle Central, September 1956

The east end of Newcastle Central Station accommodated suburban electric trains, the predecessor of the modern Metro system, and some other local services. Indeed, in 1904 the North Tyneside loop and the Riverside branch became one of the first suburban electric railways in Britain. In 1938, electric trains were introduced on the service to South Shields. Steam trains, systematically replaced by diesel multiple units from November 1955, ran down the Durham coast to Sunderland and Middlesbrough. Besides the express trains, stopping trains hauled by steam engines ran along the Northumberland coast to Berwick. Today, only old Platform Seven survives; five of the other six are used for car parking. The atmosphere of smoke and steam, the all pervading grime and the mysterious gloom have vanished. In the 1950s, the east end was always busy as the following photographs of the lost platforms illustrate.

Platforms Four to Seven (right to left), Newcastle Central, 22 April 1957

Smoke, steam and sunshine would mingle at the gloomy east end of Newcastle Central (as shown on the previous page). Below, the stopping train from Edinburgh stands at Platform Four while a new diesel unit at Platform Five has just arrived from Middlesbrough.

Class A3 60072 'Sunstar' (52B), March 1957

On the opposite page (above) a vintage North Eastern Railway G5, built at North Road Works in 1896, Victorian times, leaves for Sunderland. Below this, a parcel train waits outside the parcels office next to the Station Hotel. On p.22 (top), the image shows what was a familiar scene: racing the train was a popular game with trainspotters, here seen chasing the smoke and steam as the Edinburgh train leaves Platform Eight.

Class G5 67278 (54A), leaving Newcastle Central, 22 April 1957

Class V1 67647 (52A), Newcastle Central, 1957

Class A2/3 60516 'Hycilla' (52A), Newcastle Central, November 1956

Class A3 60099 'Call Boy' (64B), Newcastle Central, March 1957

Class A8 69893 (51C), Newcastle Central, March 1957

This photograph shows a train from Middlesbrough arriving at Platform Seven. Notice how the doors have been flung open by impatient travellers, a practice which would be impossible these days. You can make out the figure of the wheeltapper walking in the shadows, his long hammer slung over his right shoulder. Wheeltapping was a safety measure to check for cracks in the wheels. To the left, porters are unloading luggage from an electric train. The picture overleaf shows coaches being marshalled at Platform Eight. The numbering of the platforms has changed since the 1950s. Platforms 1-6 no longer exist; Platform 7 has become Platform 1, Platform 8 is now Platform 2, and so on.

Class J21 65110 (52B), Newcastle Central, 26 January 1957

Class J21 65061 (52B), Newcastle Central, November 1956

As can be seen in these photographs of Newcastle Central Station, major alterations were taking place during 1956 and 1957. Many of the awnings to carry the old roof were being removed to be replaced by a modern structure. The signalling system was also being modernised with semaphore signals being replaced by colour lights. At this time operations were controlled by three signal boxes, a huge and complicated task since the Central was one of the busiest stations outside London, handling over five hundred trains each day. In the photograph overleaf, part of the station roof has been removed and the foundations for the new signal box are suspended above the carriage sidings. When this box opened in 1959, colour light signalling controlled all train movements. Today, the scene has changed again, with new platforms for the Sunderland and Carlisle trains occupying the space where (again overleaf) a vintage D20/2 62375 is removing empty stock to Heaton carriage sidings. Note the water bag attached to its feeder pipe, a feature of railway stations at the time, essential for replenishing steam trains and found at the end of all of the main line platforms.

Class D20/2 62375 (52D), Newcastle Central, November 1956

After a distance of a quarter of a mile, this train would arrive at the other major station in Newcastle – Manors. Today there is an underground Metro station at Manors, but in the 1950s there was a large complex above ground, with nine platforms. Suburban electric trains to the coast called at Manors and the steam trains to Blyth and Newbiggin-by-the-Sea started from this station. To the north was the large New Bridge Street Goods Depot which was badly damaged by German bombs in 1941 but after refurbishment it continued in operation until 1967. The photograph opposite was taken from the north, where student accommodation now stands. It shows shunting operations in progress.

Class J72, New Bridge Street Goods Depot, 26 January 1957

What the German air raid failed to destroy was used after the war as a warehouse, mainly for fruit and vegetable traffic. In the 1980s it was demolished and a cinema complex built, now closed and demolished in its turn. Today, extensions to the University of Northumbria are being built on this site. Overleaf, a freight train passes through Manors East on a cold February afternoon, en route to Teesside; note the overhead D.C. electrification wires and supports for the Quayside branch.

On p.29 a coal train struggles with its heavy load through Platform Seven at Manors. The third rail, which carried the current for the electric passenger trains, can be seen in the foreground.

The next station along the main line was Heaton, which had opened in 1887 to replace an original station further east. This was frequented regularly by train-spotters, who used to take the electric train to Walkergate because it passed by the large engine shed at Heaton. Today, nothing remains of Heaton Station which was closed and demolished in 1980.

Class K1 62059 (51G), Manors, 5 January 1957

Class Q6 63441 (52C), Manors, 5 January 1957

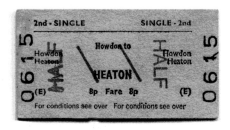

Four images around Heaton ...

The next four images are taken around Heaton: the 'Heart of Midlothian' express from Edinburgh thundering south; a light engine returning to the shed; the stopping train from Alnwick pulling away from Platform Two, and on p.32 the 'Elizabethan' heading north pulled by 'Seagull'. This service ran from London to Edinburgh non stop each weekday which was the longest run in the world by a steam engine. It was hauled by A4 Pacifics with corridor tenders to enable the crew to be changed at the half way point, between York and Northallerton.

Class A1 60162 'Saint Johnstoun' (64B), Heaton Hall Road, May 1956

Class K3/2 61952 (52D), Heaton Station, February 1956

Class D20/2 62375 (52D), Heaton Station, November 1956

Class A4 60033 'Seagull' (34A), North View, August 1956

North View and Heaton Junction were popular adjacent meeting points for train-spotters because they were on the main line and near to Heaton engine shed. The following five photographs recreate the busy scene at North View.

Class J27 65837 (52E)
North View
May 1956

Class K3/2 61904 (53A)
North View
May 1956

Class J72 68725 (52B)
North View
May 1956

Class J21 65061 (52B)
North View
March 1956

Class A3 60066 'Merry Hampton' (36A), North View, April 1956

The engine shed was a 'no go' area with entrance by means of a long path running alongside the electric line. We often risked trespassing half way down this path to see the engines parked at the west end, known as the 'dead line', which can be seen on the following page. Ironically, it is now used to give access to Chillingham Road Metro Station.

The photographs on the following pages try to recreate the atmosphere of Heaton Shed which housed shunting locomotives, freight engines and main line express engines. Permits for official visits were issued by the railway's Public Relations Officers and visits usually took place at the weekend when most of the locomotives were in sheds. Unofficial visits were possible, depending upon the shedmaster; places like Heaton and Gateshead were difficult without a permit, but others like Blyth and Tyne Dock were easy. Sheds were dirty and dangerous places but they held a great attraction for enthusiasts because of the number of engines to be seen together.

Class K2/2 61777 (38A) and Class B1 61025 'Pallah' (52D)
Heaton 'dead line', September 1956

Class D49/2 62744 'The Holderness' (62B)
Heaton 'dead line' September 1956

*Class J71 68251
(52B)
Heaton Shed
June 1956*

*Class J21 65039
(52B)
Heaton Shed
June 1956*

*Class J25 65656
(52B)
Heaton Shed
June 1956*

*Class J72 68722 (50A)
and J71 68264 (52B)
Heaton Shed
June 1956*

Ex works Class V2 60886 (52B), Heaton Shed, June 1956

However interesting it may have been to see a number of trains together in one place, to my mind it was much more exhilerating to see the engines in action as they ran through Heaton Junction and climbed Benton Bank.

The picture overleaf shows the 'Flying Scotsman' – the 10am service from King's Cross to Edinburgh. In this instance the train is being hauled by the A4 Pacific 60012 'Commonwealth of Australia' here seen tackling the climb up Benton Bank, a 'streak' in action.

Class A4 60012 'Commonwealth of Australia' (64B), Benton Bank, July 1956

The following five photographs of steam engines, hard at work climbing Benton Bank to Little Benton, capture the magic of steam. They show the Alnwick train, a local freight, the stopping train to Edinburgh and two views of the 'Queen of Scots' Pullman, one of the luxury expresses of the day.

Class D20/1, Benton Bank, circa October 1957

Class J27 65799 (52E)
Benton Bank
September 1956

Class B1 61244 'Strang Steel' (64B)
Benton Bank
September 1956

Class AI climbing Benton Bank, August 1956

Class AI climbing Benton Bank, August 1956

The picture below shows a freight engine and guard's van leaving Little Benton sidings for Heaton. This was where our gang met most evenings after school and was popularly known as Redhill after the disused pitheap of Bigges Main Colliery, seen behind the tree. The much larger pit heap is that of the Rising Sun Colliery at Wallsend which was still at work in the mid 1950s. This industrial landscape has now been eradicated: the Rising Sun is a nature reserve and our adventure playground, Redhill, has been converted into a BMX track. Bushes and scrub now cover the sidings and suburban housing has replaced the farmers' fields.

Class J27 65780 (52E), Little Benton South

Train-spotting was an all year round activity. Even when heavy snow covered the main line, enthusiasts ventured out to see the expresses working through Little Benton, as shown in the pictures overleaf.

Southbound
Class V2
Little Benton
March 1958

Northbound
Class A1
Little Benton
March 1958

We all had our favourite locomotives and mine was the D20 illustrated in the next two phographs as it pulled the Alnwick train through Little Benton. Built at Gateshead Works for the North Eastern Railway, these locomotives had once hauled the fastest expresses in the country.

Class D20/2 62375
(52D)
Little Benton North

*Class D20/2 62375
(52D)
Little Benton South*

I will never forget the sheer joy of standing on the bridge at Little Benton South when an express train was speeding towards me. In the photograph below you can see this, as the London train races south past the sidings.

Class A1 60153 'Flamboyant' (50A), Little Benton South

On the next page a stopping train for Edinburgh approaches Little Benton North signal box. Both the signal cabins and the sidings are long gone, and the locations overgrown.

Class B1 61014 'Oribi' (52D), Little Benton North

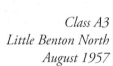

Class A3
Little Benton North
August 1957

Class A2
Benton Quarry
August 1956

On the previous page an evening express from Edinburgh approaches Little Benton North. Another express from Edinburgh passes, this time through Benton Quarry, (bottom) which was an important junction with the line from Manors to the coast. Forest Hall Station was opened in 1856 and closed not long after its centenary in 1958. The photographs show the 'Queen of Scots' Pullman and a local coal train, both heading south through Forest Hall.

Class A3 60041 'Salmon Trout' (64B) hauling the 'North Briton' Forest Hall January 1957

LMS Class 4MT 43101 (52B) Forest Hall January 1957

The photograph overleaf (top) shows the train from Alnwick arriving at Killingworth Station: you can see the ticket collector on the far right of the picture. The train service to Killingworth ended in 1958. We often caught the bus from Heaton to Killingworth to travel in style to the Central Station for a day's train-spotting. Killingworth Station marked the end of our home patch.

Class D20/1 62396 (52D), Killingworth, September 1957, heading south

Class D20/2 62375 (52D), Killingworth, January 1957, heading north

EXPEDITIONS ON A BICYCLE

The Redhill Gang were mobile and we frequently went by bicycle on expeditions from the home patch in search of engines. Young lads, we would set off on our bikes with packed lunches in our pockets for long journeys with no adult supervision or protection, in a way that would seem unthinkable today.

The Redhill Gang at Little Benton South, August 1956

One favourite spot was the Weetslade Coal Depot near Gosforth Park where there was often the opportunity to ride on the tank engines belonging to the Coal Board. The picture overleaf shows two of the gang on the footplate. The area is now a nature reserve.

All of the collieries in the neighbourhood had a fleet of tank engines and most were within easy range for an evening's cycle ride. We used to make visits after school to Seaton Delaval Works, Seghill Colliery and Backworth Colliery in the hope of getting a ride in the cab of a locomotive.

NCB 0-4-0 Saddletank
Weetslade Depot
August 1956

NCB No. 42
Weetslade Depot
August 1956

NCB No. 40
Weetslade Depot
August 1956

NCB No. 29
Hartley
1958

NCB No. 27
Hartley
1958

NCB No. 24, Hartley, 1958

NCB No. 60
Backworth
1959

NCB No. 27
Hartley
1958

NCB No. 29
Backworth
1959

Class V1 67647
(52B)
approaching Seghill
1957

NCB No. 41, Seghill, August 1956

NCB No. 28, Seghill, 1956

The Blyth and Tyne Railway was within easy reach of Newcastle which made it a popular place to visit at weekends. There were two sheds at Blyth and none of the officials there objected to our visits.

The chain ferry across the River Blyth

The wonderful ferry linking the two sites, shown above in a photograph taken in 1957, was an added attraction. Both of the sheds housed freight locomotives to handle the important coal traffic from the neighbouring collieries. They also stabled shunting engines which worked on the coal staithes, which were the heavy wooden platforms built out into the river so that the coal could be tipped from the wagons into the sea going colliers.

The vintage G5 tank engines which operated the push and pull trains were stabled at South Blyth. One of these can be seen at the top of the opposite page, leaving Blyth Station pushing the coaches towards Newsham. On such occasions the fireman was left on the engine footplate and the driver sat in a special compartment at the head of the front coach. The driver's cab can be seen in the empty carriage on the right hand side.

Class G5 67340 (52F) leaving Blyth, January 1957

Class G5 67281 (52F)
August 1956

Class G5 67323 (52F)
Class J77 68424 (52F)
August 1956

I took these photographs of passenger tank locos and shunting engines during a visit to South Blyth engine sheds.

Class J 27: 65797, 65794, 65867 and Q6 63399, North Blyth Shed (52F), August 1956

The roundhouse was a popular type of shed with the North Eastern Railway. The engines were grouped around a turntable which made them more accessible than they would have been in a straight shed. On the previous page we see four engines around the central turntable at North Blyth.

Class G5 67340 (52F), Seaton Deleval Hall, 1957

The Avenue branch ran from Monkseaton to Hartley and these photographs show the push and pull passenger train first pulling northwards towards Hartley (above) and then pushing from Hartley (below).

*Class G5 67340
(52F)
leaving Hartley
1957*

Note the driver in the right hand front window.

Class G5 67340 (52F) leaving Hartley, February 1957

Hartley Station is illustrated below. The train from Monkseaton has arrived, en route to Blyth. There are no passengers waiting at the station.

Class G5 67281 (52F), Hartley Station, September 1957

Below you can see coal trains diverging to follow the main line towards Seghill, Percy Main and the Tyne Commission Quay. It was a cold February afternoon in 1957 when these photographs were taken, hence the dark shadows and steam effects.

Class J27 65807
(52E)
Hartley Station
February 1957

Class J27 65864
(52B)
Hartley Station
February 1957

Over the page are some views of Newsham, which was a busy station. It handled trains from Newbiggin to Manors and Monkseaton to Blyth as well as the constant flow of coal traffic. It was always a good idea to take a photograph of the train crew in the hope of being asked onto the footplate for a ride. Although engaged in a filthy job, both the driver and his young fireman are smartly dressed, as you can see from the photograph on p.59.

Class V3 67685 (52B), Newsham, September 1957

Class G5 67281 (52F), Newsham, September 1957

*Crew of Class G5
67281 (52F)
Newsham
September 1957
Note that they are wearing
ties, railway caps and
polished shoes!*

Class J27 65858 (52E), Newsham, September 1957

The Blyth and Tyne system was closed to passenger traffic in 1964, despite serving the large towns of Ashington and Blyth, each with a population of around 30,000 people. The picture below shows the train from Newbiggin-by-the-Sea at North Seaton Station, which was demolished in 1972. Interestingly, at the time of writing there are proposals for re-instating services from Blyth and Ashington to Newcastle.

Class G5 67341 (52F), North Seaton, February 1957

Class Q6 63403 (52F) near Woodhorn, February 1957

Freight traffic was the lifeblood of the Blyth and Tyne Railway. On a cold February day in 1957 a coal train strains with a heavy load from Lynemouth Colliery (above) while further south a train of mixed goods is also struggling (below). Although closed to passengers, the line remains open for freight traffic – the main customer being the Alcan aluminium smelter.

Class J27 65864 (52B) near Newsham, January 1957

The next three images depict the scene at the station of Newbiggin-by-the-Sea, once a popular seaside resort. British Railways had converted several carriages into camping coaches; parked in a siding at the station they provided additional holiday accomodation. The G5 67431 engine is not fitted with push and pull and therefore has to run round its train for the return journey (below); in the photograph opposite it is engaged in a shunting operation watched by the station porter. The large station building is hidden by steam as the G5 prepares to leave (p.64). These G5 tank engines were built at Darlington and they were the mainstay of branch line traffic in the North East. Nothing of this railway scene at Newbiggin has survived.

Class G5 67341 (52F), Newbiggin, February 1957

Class G5 67341 (52F), Newbiggin, February 1957

Class G5 67341 (52F), Newbiggin, February 1957

The Tyne Valley was a popular destination for a cycle ride. The Newcastle to Carlisle Railway is still open but it has changed greatly since the mid 1950s, as is evident from the next set of photographs. At that time, the principal route ran from the Central Station, through Scotswood, and on via Blaydon to Hexham and Carlisle. An alternative route diverged at Scotswood, where there were two stations, and followed the route of the old Wylam waggonway, past George Stephenson's cottage, to join the main route at West Wylam Junction. It crossed the River Tyne on a bridge remarkably like the more famous Tyne Bridge built fifty-two years later. For much of its route this line is now a country park.

The photograph below shows a stopping train from Hexham via North Wylam heading for Scotswood through the lost landscape of coal mining west of Lemington.

Class V1 67639 (52C) near Lemington, June 1956

In the February twilight of 1957, a local train service runs towards the station at Heddon-on-the-Wall (top) to be followed by an express train from Carlisle (bottom). The station at Heddon, situated one mile from the village, was closed in 1958.

Class 4MT approaching Heddon-on-the-Wall, February 1957

Class V2 approaching Heddon-on-the-Wall, February 1957

BY BIKE TO BRAMPTON

I undertook one of my most ambitious bicycle adventures in October 1956. The first stage was a bike ride from Newcastle to Brampton where I left my bike at the station and returned to Newcastle by train. The following weekend I returned to Brampton by train, collected my bike and cycled back to Newcastle via Alston. What follows is a photographic record of those journeys.

Class V2 60967 (52A), approaching Wylam, 20 October 1956

In this first photograph, an express passenger train for Carlisle speeds through Wylam Station which is still open today to passenger traffic. Overleaf, as a 'through' train the morning commuter train from Hexham didn't make a stop at Riding Mill. This pretty station was typical of the many delightful stations on the line, like Stocksfield, Gilsland and Greenhead as illustrated on the following pages.

Tank Engine passing through Riding Mill, 20 October 1956

Below is a view of Stocksfield Station, which is still open, although a car-park has replaced the Goods Yard. Thousands of tourists from Tyneside used to travel by train to Gilsland to visit the famous Spa Hotel, which was where Sir Walter Scott met his wife in 1797. Named from the sulphurous spring nearby, the hotel remains open but the station (opposite top) closed in 1967.

Stocksfield Station looking east, 20 October 1956

Gilsland Station looking east, 20 October 1956

There has been a reawakening of interest in walking the length of Hadrian's Wall since the opening of the official path in 2002, and there must be many walkers who regret that Greenhead Station (below) closed in 1967.

Greenhead Station looking south, 20 October 1956

Corbridge Station is illustrated in the next two photographs. The first shows the view looking west towards Dilston with the goods yard on the left. Bottom, the view to the east with the local pick-up freight arriving.

Corbridge Station looking west, 20 October 1956

Class J39/2 64842 (52C), Corbridge, 20 October 1956

Class B1, passing Widehaugh, east of Hexham

On the previous page you can see the train from Carlisle to Newcastle in a photograph taken east of Hexham. The image below shows shunting operations taking place in the coal yard at Hexham. These sidings are now a car park. The locomotive, Class J21 65033, built by the North Eastern Railways, has been preserved and can be seen at Beamish Museum. Note that the engine is fitted with a snow plough.

Class J21 65033 (52C) at Hexham

On the next page is an image which captures the atmosphere as the pick up freight storms away from Warden Paper Mill.

Class J39/2 64842 (52C), Warden, 20 October 1956

Class B1 61290 (68E): the morning train to Newcastle leaving Fourstones, 20 October 1956

Coal trains were a familiar sight in the region until the decline of the coal industry in the early 1980s. Here a coal train heads west from Haltwhistle towards Carlisle.

Class K1 62002 (52C) near Haltwhistle, 20 October 1956

This photograph, taken on the same October day, shows a Class A3 at full throttle, thundering through Low Row on its way from Carlisle to Newcastle with a passenger train.

Class K1, Upper Denton Crossing near Gilsland, 20 October 1956

Above, in the twilight of the autumn evening, a coal train can be seen bustling through the Irthing Valley towards Gilsland, perhaps loaded with limestone for ICI Prudhoe. Below you can see a mixed goods train as it hurries through Brampton Junction.

Class K1, Brampton Junction, 20 October 1956

Class K1 passing through Brampton Junction, 27 October 1956

This peaceful view is of Brampton Junction looking east, again in October 1956. It was here that the booking clerk, Thomas Edmundson, invented the cardboard ticket as illustrated on page nine, a design which was used throughout Britain until the 1960s.

The turntable, water column and curved platform on the right at Haltwhistle (above) were for services to Alston. This branch line crossed over the River South Tyne by means of the bridge that can be made out on the top far right of the picture.

This beautiful line was opened in 1852 and climbed 500ft (152.4m) in thirteen miles to Alston, the highest market town in the country. The bottom picture and the one overleaf show the station and shed at Alston. The line was closed in 1976, but it has since been replaced between Alston and Kirkhaugh by a privately owned, narrow gauge railway, and there are plans to extend the line to Slaggyford. Immediately below is a view of the station at Slaggyford in 1956.

BR Class 3 77014 (52C), Alston Station, 27 October 1956

BR Class 3 77014 (52C), Alston Station, 27 October 1956

ON BIKES SOUTH OF THE TYNE

Another favourite weekend cycle ride was to the south of the Tyne using the new pedestrian tunnel under the river, which had the longest escalator in the country. The engine shed at Tyne Dock housed some of the most powerful freight engines in the country, such as the North Eastern Railway's class Q7 (below).

Class Q7 63474 (54B), Tyne Dock, August 1956

Also stabled at Tyne Dock were the WDs, purchased from the War Department (overleaf) and the newly built 9Fs of British Rail, which can be seen on the following two photographs. These engines were used on the heavy freight trains from the docks, especially on the iron ore trains to Consett.

Class WD 90026 (54B), Tyne Dock, August 1956

Class 9F 92060 (54B), Tyne Dock, August 1956
Showing the Westinghouse pumps fitted to operate the iron ore hoppers.

Class 9F 92061 (54B), Tyne Dock, August 1956

The photograph on the previous page shows the driver at the cab door of a 9F; as you can see he is dwarfed by the massive engine, which would weigh 140 tons. The image below gives us a rare glimpse inside Tyne Dock shed, showing cleaners at work on this J71 shunting engine used in the docks.

Class J71 68265 (54B), Tyne Dock Shed, August 1957

Tyne Dock had a railway station (overleaf top) which was served by electric trains from Newcastle and by steam trains working the South Shields to Sunderland service. This station was closed in 1981 and a new station was built for the Metro. However, High Shields, another station on this route (overleaf bottom), was bypassed by the Metro which took a different route between Tyne Dock and South Shields. This area is now served by Chichester Metro Station.

Class G5 approaching Tyne Dock Station, March 1957

Class G5 67265 (54A), High Shields Station, March 1957

To the left you can see the train from Sunderland arriving at South Shields Station and (below) the G5 tank engine running around its coaches for the return journey. This impressive station was closed in 1981 and its replacement, the Metro Station, is 100 yards to the south.

Class G5 67248 (54A), South Shields, March 1957

Class G5 67248 seen on the previous page is now at the head of the train for the return journey to Sunderland, and an electric unit for Newcastle waits in the other platform. Taking this portrait of the driver and fireman paid dividends: I was invited onto the footplate for the ride to Sunderland and actually allowed to operate the brake. At Sunderland I had to hide from the traffic inspector and was dropped off in Fawcett Park to escape detection. Imagine that happening today!

To the left you can see the train from South Shields near Boldon.

Class G5 67278 (54A), 12 January 1957

Class G5 67248 (54A), Sunderland Station, March 1957

The photo above shows a scene at Sunderland Station in the Spring of 1957 with a train for Newcastle departing from Platform Three. Note that the porter is sprinkling water to keep the dust down. The station, which had four platforms, was below ground level, in a culvert. Today, the scene is completely different: the station has been rebuilt underground with only two platforms, and the lines are shared with the Metro trains from Newcastle. The Metro extension runs to South Hylton and follows the course of the former Sunderland to Durham line. For most of the journey between Sunderland and Gateshead, the Metro trains follow the route taken by the steam trains in 1957 – the course of the old Brandling Junction Railway. But in the age of steam it was a very different journey, as the images on the following pages show.

Class A8 69893 (51C), East Boldon Station, 12 January 1957

Above you can see the train for Sunderland leaving East Boldon Station. This was an attractive rural station in the mid 1950s, with well kept flower beds. Note the gas lighting and the signal box controlling the level crossing. Another Sunderland train is shown below near East Boldon.

Class V3 67690 (52A), near East Boldon, 12 January 1957

Class V2 60809 'The Snapper' (52A), near Pelaw, March 1957

These photographs show an industrial landscape around Pelaw, now completely lost. A Newcastle-Liverpool express passes Springwell Brickworks (above) and below a Middlesbrough-Newcastle express runs through Pelaw Junction.

Class V1 or V3 tank engine, Pelaw, March 1957

Class WD, Pelaw, March 1957

The photograph above shows the scene at Pelaw Station where a freight train of wagons for carrying steel returns to Teeside and a passenger train leaves for Middlesbrough. Pelaw was a town which emerged largely because of the Co-operative Wholesale Society and some of its factories can be seen on the right of the photographs. These are now closed.

Class V1 67639 (52C), Pelaw, March 1957

Class A5/2 69830 (51A), Pelaw, March 1957

In the top photograph you can see a morning train for Newcastle waiting at Pelaw Station. Below, a freight train heads westward beneath the covered walkway giving access to the station. The station was closed in 1979 and in the original plan for the Metro there was to be no station at Pelaw, but the present station was added in 1985.

Class Q6 63400 (54C), Pelaw, March 1957

*Class A8 69893 (51C)
leaving Gateshead West,
March 1957*

When these photographs
were taken in 1957, there
were two railway stations
in Gateshead town, both
of which were at the south
end of the High Level
Bridge, which spanned the
River Tyne as it does today.

*BR Standard Class 5MT 73161 (52A)
leaving High Level Bridge
March 1957*

These two photographs show a light engine from the locomotive depot
passing through Gateshead West to Newcastle Central and an excursion
train about to enter Gateshead East. On the opposite page the train for
Middlesbrough struggles on the wet rails to leave Gateshead East. Neither
of these stations exists today. The underground Metro station is a short
distance to the south.

Class A8 69853 (54A), leaving Gateshead East, March 1957

To the west of the stations was Greenesfield Works. Although by 1957 it serviced only small locomotives, it had formerly been the principal engineering centre of the North Eastern Railway. The works plate (shown here) from D20/1 62355 is a reminder of that period. Beyond there was the large locomotive depot where the engines for the east coast main line passenger trains were stabled. All of this is now gone and the site has been redeveloped as a housing estate.

Class A4 60002 'Sir Murrough Wilson' (52A) and Class A4 60021 'Wild Swan' (34A), Gateshead Depot, Spring 1956

Class J72 68675 (52A), Greenesfield Works, Spring 1956

Class A1 60138 'Boswell' (50A) and A2/3 60521 'Watling Street', (52A) Gateshead, 1956

97

We loved to cycle to Low Fell to watch the expresses thunder past the site of the old railway station. Immediately below can be seen the colliery waggonway that ran through the Team Valley carrying coal from the Ravenswood Drift mine to Dunston staith. The bottom photograph shows a local freight train leaving Low Fell Yard.

NCB 0-6-0 'Derwent', Team Valley, November 1956

Class J25 65728 (54C), Low Fell Yard, November 1956

SOCIETY VISITS

After the Second World War there was a great increase in the number of railway enthusiasts. The two principal railway societies were long established: the S.L.S. (Stephenson Locomotive Society) founded in 1909 and the R.C.T.S. (Railway Correspondence and Travel Society) founded in 1928. These societies promoted an academic interest in all aspects of the railway, holding regular meetings throughout the country and publishing monthly magazines. The Ian Allan organisation catered for the more general enthusiast and published a monthly magazine '*Trains Illustrated*' and, twice annually, the '*A.B.C. of British Locomotives*' containing a complete list of all locomotives in service. Indeed, this and Allan's earlier books, which were self-published, could be described as the catalyst that brought about the birth of train-spotting as popular hobby. He also published a separate, complementary shed book which listed where these locomotives were stabled. The books were so successful that Allan and his wife fostered railway clubs. An Ian Allan Locospotters Club met in the east end of Newcastle in a rented room near Heaton Station, encouraging interest in railways through regular meetings and visits to railway centres and their engine sheds.

Class A5/2 69833 (51A), Darlington, June 1956

Each month the Redhill Gang visited Darlington Shed and Works using links with the R.C.T.S. The photograph opposite (top) shows the shed yard dominated by the coaling plant. Those following illustrate the variety of locomotives to be seen at the shed. Each shed was given a code number (Darlington was 51A) and each locomotive carried a shed plate on the smokebox door to indicate its home depot. These plates are now collectors' items. Note the number of locomotives in pristine condition, fresh from a major service at North Road Works – like the J73 68361 from Hull at the bottom of p.102.

LMS Class 2MT 46475 (51A), Darlington Shed, December 1956

Class J77 68430 (52F)
Darlington Shed
9 June 1956

Class G5 67284 (51A)
Darlington, June 1956

*BR Class 3MT 82028
(51A)
Darlington
early 1956*

*Class J77 68410
(51A)
Darlington
early 1956*

*Class J77 68423
(51A)
Darlington
early 1956*

*Class J73 68361
(53C)
Darlington
24 March 1956*

Class V2 60959 (64B), Darlington, 24 March 1956

Class B1 61151 (39B), Darlington, 24 March 1956

Class B16/3 61444 (50A), Darlington, early 1956

BR Class 2MT 78016 (51H), Bank Top Station, October 1956

There were two stations at Darlington. The main line station is Bank Top, where in the photograph above the 10.10am train for Penrith waits to depart from Platform Five. The other station is North Road, its buildings now a museum. The bottom photograph shows the train from Middleton-in-Teesdale waiting at North Road Station.

Class G5 67305 (51A), North Road Station, September 1957

In 1910, the Chief Mechanical Engineer of the North Eastern Railway moved to Darlington, after which North Road Works replaced Greenesfield as the principal workshop of the railway company. These photographs were taken in 1956 – ten years before its closure. They show a line of engine frames outside the erecting shops and a tank engine en route to the boiler shops

Class J25
65720 (51D)
65656 (52B)
65687 (52B)
65675 (52B)
North Road Works
9 December 1956

Class J72
North Road Works
9 December 1956

The scrap yard where redundant engines were broken up was also part of the works. Such was our concern for our favourite locomotives that we even attempted to buy them, but not surprisingly, the price was far beyond the purse of teenage lads, as you can see from the letter I received from British Railways in November 1956 (p.109). Interestingly, a preservation society is currently (2007) trying to rebuild a G5 tank engine.

Class N5 69317
(9F)
Darlington Scrap Yard
24 March 1956

Class J71 68297
(50A)
Darlington Scrap Yard
9 June 1956

Class N5
Darlington Scrap Yard
9 June 1956

Class J77 68407
(51E)
Darlington Scrap Yard
February 1956

Class D20/1 62387 (52D), Darlington Scrap Yard, 1 September 1957

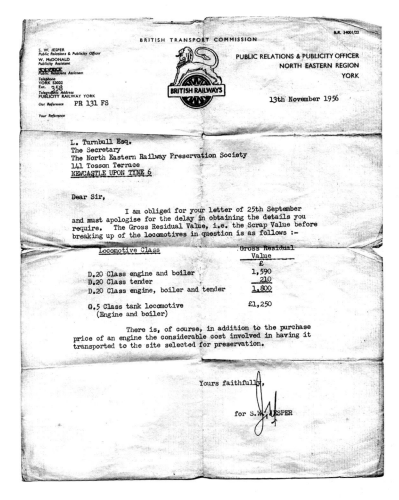

There were other society trips that took us much further away – to Edinburgh, Carlisle, Humberside, Manchester and South Yorkshire. These were essentially number-collecting jaunts, where the objective was to visit as many sheds in a day as time and energy permitted. For example, on Sunday 13 May 1956 we visited not only Doncaster shed and works but Selby, Normanton, Mexborough and Goole too. The photographs on the following pages illustrate that journey.

Class B17/4 61652 'Darlington' (31A), Doncaster Shed, May 1956

Doncaster was the locomotive works of the Great Northern Railway and some very famous locomotives had been built there, such as 'Mallard' the fastest steam engine in the world and 'The Flying Scotsman', perhaps the most famous steam engine of them all. Although only a hundred miles away, Doncaster housed engines that we didn't see in the North East, as these photographs show.

Class J69 68507 (30A) Doncaster Shed May 1956

Class N2/4 69587 (34B), Doncaster Shed, May 1956

Class D11/1 62660 'Butler Henderson' (40A), Doncaster Shed, May 1956

Class J6 64196 (34B), Doncaster Shed, May 1956

Class B17/4 61647 'Helmingham Hall' (32B), Doncaster Shed, May 1956

The next four images, taken at Doncaster Works, show a newly serviced locomotive (opposite) and the three departmental engines belonging to the works. The locomotive immediately below is unusual – it is a Sentinel Engine.

Class Y3 68181
Doncaster Works No. 3
May 1956

Class J52/2 68816
Doncaster Works No. 2
May 1956

Class J52/2 68845
Doncaster Works No. 1
May 1956

Class B1 61331 (34A), Doncaster Works, May 1956

These photographs are of heavy freight locomotives on display: ex War Department engine 90670 at Selby, and London Midland and Scottish 8F locomotive 48357 at Normanton motive power depot.

Class WD 90670 (50C), Selby, May 1956

LMS Class 8F 48357 (20D), Normanton, May 1956

Edinburgh was always a popular place for society visits and for day trips by the family. Today there are two major stations in the city, but at that time there were three: Waverley, dominated by the North British Railway Hotel, Haymarket to the west and the Caledonian Railway's Princess Street Station at the end of Lothian Road, which no longer exists. However, the Caledonian Hotel is still in business.

Class A3 60089 'Felstead' (64B), Edinburgh Waverley, July 1957

Class A3, Edinburgh Haymarket, July 1957

One favourite spot for train-spotters was the bridge over the main line in Princess Street Gardens, which is still used today. In fact, it now has a perspex parapet to give young enthusiasts a better view. These photographs were taken from the bridge. Above opposite a local passenger service heads west followed by an express train (this page, below). Opposite (bottom) the Aberdeen fish train heads east, the Caledonian Hotel in the background.

Class A1 60161 'North British' (64B), Princess Street Gardens, 1958

Class D49, Princess Street Gardens, 1958

Class A3, Princess Street Gardens, 1958

There were three locomotive depots in Edinburgh – Haymarket, Dalry Road and St Margaret's, the latter being illustrated on these two pages. The shed was in two parts: to the south of the east coast main line was the most important part of the depot, while across the main line to the north was accommodation for smaller tank engines. The photograph below shows an engine leaving the main depot. At the bottom of this page you can see the station pilot travelling along the main line with coaches from Waverley, while the shed foreman waits to cross.

Class K2/2 61775 'Loch Treig' (65A), St Margaret's, May 1956

Class J83 68477 (64A), St Margaret's, May 1956

In the northern part of the depot the tank engines were left in the open. Many of these were shunting engines from Leith Docks such as the delightful little 'Pugs' shown in the photographs below. Incredible as it may seem today in a world awash with health and safety regulations, train-spotters wandered merrily between the two halves of St Margaret's shed, dodging the traffic of the main line.

*Class Y9 68102
(64A)
St Margaret's
May 1956*

*Caledonian 'Pug'
56035 (64A)
St Margaret's
May 1956*

*Class J88
68320
(64A)
St Margaret's
May 1956*

Class N15
69152 (64A)
St Margaret's
May 1956

Class Y9
68119 (64A)
St Margaret's
May 1956

Class Y9
68099 (64A)
St Margaret's
May 1956

Carlisle Citadel Station on the west coast main line was a Mecca for railway enthusiasts, especially on holiday weekends because of the variety of locomotives which they could see there. Engines arrived from the south, apparently exhausted after the strenuous climb up Shap. To the north they faced the climb up Beattock (mentioned in WH Auden's famous poem *The Night Mail*).

Pulling up Beattock, a steady climb –
The gradient's against her but she's on time.

Because of these gradients, many trains were double-headed, that is pulled by two engines, which added to the excitement. The images on this and the next three pages show the range of engines to be seen at the south of the station in April 1956.

LMS 'Jubilee' Class 45666 'Cornwallis' (12A), Carlisle, April 1956

BR 'Clan' Class 72003 'Clan Fraser', Carlisle, April 1956

LMS Class 2P 40602 (68A), Carlisle, April 1956

LMS Class 5 45197 (12A), Carlisle, April 1956

LMS Class 6P 45551 'Patriot' (12A), Carlisle, April 1956

LMS Class 8P 46223 'Princess Alice' (66A), Kingmoor, April 1956

There were three principal locomotive depots in Carlisle. Kingmoor (68A), and its sub-shed at Durran Hill and Upperby (12A) housed engines of the former London, Midland and Scottish Railway for the west coast main line. One such was the 'Princess Alice', one of the most powerful locomotives in Britain, illustrated on the previous page at Kingmoor. The fourth shed was Canal (68E); it stabled engines of the former North British Railway and the London North Eastern Railway which worked the Waverley Route to Edinburgh via Hawick.

These images show freight engines at Kingmoor (below) and passenger locos at Upperby (opposite top) waiting their turn of duty.

Caledonian
Class 3F 57653
(68A)
Kingmoor
April 1956

LMS
Class 3F 43301
(68A)
Kingmoor
April 1956

LMS Class 2P 40669 (67D), Upperby, April 1956

Meanwhile, at Canal shed (below) an LNER express loco 'Flamingo' and a NBR passenger engine 'Dugald Dalgetty' are also waiting.

Class A3 60095
'Flamingo' (68E)
Canal Shed
August 1956

Class D30/2 62423
'Dugald Dalgetty' (64G)
Canal Shed
August 1956

The influence of the major railway societies was so powerful that they were able to organise major excursions hauled by locomotives of their choice. This page illustrates the visit of the Stephenson Locomotive Society and the Manchester Locomotive Society to the North East in September 1956. The recently built Britannia locomotive 'Charles Dickens' has arrived with an excursion and the vintage North Eastern engines wait to take over. Below, the two veterans depart for a tour of West Durham.

Britannia Class 70033 'Charles Dickens' (9A) and Class G5 67284 (51A) Darlington, September 1956

Class G5 67284 (51A), Class B16/1 61443 (50A), Darlington, September 1956

THE RUNABOUT TICKET

Railway society tours were too expensive for the ordinary train-spotter but there was a cheaper alternative in the form of the Runabout Ticket. These were issued by the regional railways and allowed unlimited travel in a specific area for a given period – generally one week. They were intended to enable people to have a cheap holiday by using the rail network. These tickets were very popular in the 1950s – a time when cars were owned only by the few. The name of the game for railway enthusiasts was to travel as much as possible on a Runabout Ticket, even if they ended up by being completely exhausted.

Class G5 67343 (54A), Durham, 3 September 1957

In September 1957 I bought a ticket which covered all of County Durham apart from the main line between Newcastle Central and Durham City, and in four days I travelled (alone) over five hundred miles for 6s 3d, which is 32p! An image of my ticket is reproduced here. This chapter records the railway scenes in the area covered by the ticket. Most of the photographs were taken at the time of that holiday.

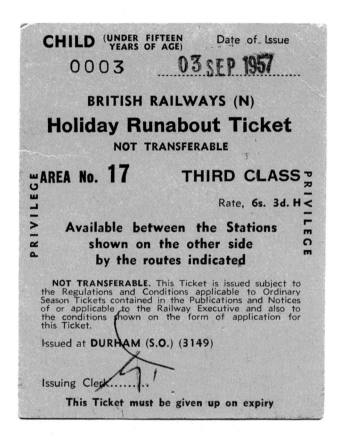

Examples of the journeys I made are listed below. The number of the engine hauling the train is recorded, as is the distance travelled in miles. 'FP' stands for footplate ride – a greatly prized experience as you can imagine.

Itinerary for Tuesday 3 September 1957

		Miles
60033	Newcastle to Durham	14.25
69875	Durham to Bishop Auckland	11.00
46482	Bishop Auckland to Crook	6.00
46482	Crook to Bishop Auckland	6.00
46482 and 69850	Bishop Auckland to Shildon	3.50
69841	Shildon to Beechburn	7.75
69841	Beechburn to Bishop Auckland	4.25
67329	Bishop Auckland to Durham	11.00
60091	Durham to Newcastle	14.25

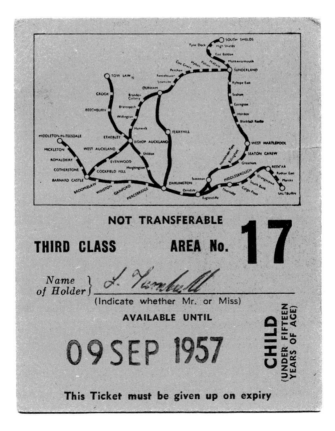

Itinerary for Wednesday 4 September 1957

		Miles
60121	Newcastle to Darlington	36.50
46481 and 69856	Darlington to Bishop Auckland	12.50
67248	Bishop Aukland to Durham	11.00
67320	Durham to Sunderland (FP)	15.00
69874	Sunderland to South Shields	7.75
69874	South Shields to Sunderland	7.75
DMU	Sunderland to West Hartlepool	18.25
60963	West Hartlepool to Sunderland	18.25
67343	Sunderland to Durham	15.00
60069	Durham to Newcastle	14.25

Here you can see contrasting scenes at Durham City. Below, a coal train storms up the bank while (opposite top) a vintage G5 struggles to depart with the train for Bishop Auckland. Opposite (middle) both engine and driver are taking a rest at Bishop Auckland Station. Opposite (bottom) the train for Darlington is preparing to leave Crook Station.

Class B1 61353 (51A), Durham, 3 September 1957

Class G5 67343
(54A)
Durham
4 September 1957

Class G5 67329
(54A)
Bishop Auckland
4 September 1957

LMS Class 2MT
46482
(51F)
Crook
3 September 1957

This was an everyday scene in the North East – a coal train being shunted. Note the concentration of the driver in the cab and the guard with the shunting pole for uncoupling wagons. But also note the children on the bridge, bathing in the engine's steam.

Class J26 65731 (51F), Beechburn, 4 September 1957

This photograph was taken near Beechburn Station and shows the train from Crook arriving.

Class A5/2 69841 (51A), Beechburn, 4 September 1957

Class A8 69856 (51F), Etherley, 4 September 1957

Etherley was the next station down the line. Above, a train from Crook arrives at Etherley en route for Bishop Auckland, Shildon and Darlington. Shildon was then a railway town with a large wagon works; today, the station is in the centre of the National Railway Museum's reserve collection. The images on the next two pages recreate the busy scene at Shildon in the days of steam. Freight trains are moving about the station while a shunting engine wanders through followed by a passenger train for Crook. Today, none of the freight traffic survives.

Class V2 60955
(61B)
Shildon
3 September 1957

Class A8 69850 (54A) and LMS Class 2MT 46482 (51F), Shildon, 3 September 1957

Class J39/1 64848 (51F), Shildon, 3 September 1957

Class J72 69018
(51F)
Shildon
3 September 1957

Class A5/2 69841
(51A)
Shildon
4 September 1957

The single line branch railway from Barnard Castle to Middleton-in-Teesdale was one of the most picturesque in the region. On this page, the train for Darlington waits to depart from Middleton. There was also a service to Durham and Sunderland via Bishop Auckland, with excursion trains during the summer holidays. This line closed to passengers in 1964.

Class G5 67305
(51A)
Middleton
5 September 1957

Class G5 67305 (51A), Middleton-in-Teesdale, 5 September 1957

Amid the Pennine landscape an excursion train leaves Romaldkirk while (bottom) an early evening train for Bishop Aukland approaches Mickleton in the twilight gloom.

Class L1 67705 (32B), Romaldkirk, 26 May 1958

Class A8 69875 (51F), Mickleton, 26 May 1958

The last station up the branch line was at Cotherstone. An evening train is arriving from Middleton (top) following an excursion train returning to Teesside (bottom). Another railway – the route from Barnard Castle across Stainmore to Kirkby Stephen – was a short walk away at the next village of Lartington.

Class A8 69858 (54A), Cotherstone, 26 May 1958

BR Class 3 77002 (51F), near Mickleton, 26 May 1958

Opposite (top) Photograph of the scene at Lartington as a train arrives from Darlington.

Opposite (bottom) A train-spotter watching as a train passes through Lartington.

BR Class 3 82028 (51A), Lartington, 26 May 1958

BR Class 3 82026 (51H), Lartington, 26 May 1958

Class G5 67305 (51A), Broomielaw, 5 September 1957

These photographs are of Broomielaw Station. The Middleton-Darlington push and pull train is arriving (above). Below, the train from Darlington to Penrith departs.

BR Class 82026 (51H), Broomielaw, 5 September 1957

This page shows the scene at Gainford later in the day. The train from Penrith returns, while the push and pull train to Middleton arrives from Darlington with the engine pulling.

BR Class 3 82028 (51A), Gainford, 5 September 1957

Class G5 67305 (51A), Gainford, 5 September 1957

The next two images are of the delightful country railway station at Piercebridge, where the Middleton push and pull leaves for Darlington followed by a freight train from the west. Nothing remains of the station except the station house.

Class G5 67305 (51A), Piercebridge, 5 September 1957

LMS Class 2MT 46474 (51A), Piercebridge, 5 September 1957

There was a contrasting scene further east on industrial Teesside. A steel train takes the Northallerton line at Eaglescliffe (top) while another bypasses Middlesbrough Station on the Up Goods Line. In the background are the imposing cranes of the docks.

WD leaving Eaglescliffe, November 1956

Class J26 65757 (51B), Middlesbrough, November 1956

The line to Saltburn used to be busy with suburban traffic and with excursion trains to the coast. A Middlesbrough train waits at Redcar Central (top) while (bottom) another travels from Redcar towards the coast. On the opposite page, an excursion train runs into Redcar East (top) hauled by two engines. A local service enters Marske Station on a bleak day (centre). The bottom picture shows a train for Middlesbrough waiting to leave the impressive station at Saltburn.

Class A8 69876 (51D), Redcar Central, 22 April 1957

Class A8 69854 (51D), near Redcar Central, 22 April 1957

Class D49/2s
62758
'The Cattistock'
(50D)
62727 'The Quorn'
(50D)
Redcar East
22 April 1957

Class A8
69875
(51F)
Marske
22 April 1957

Class A8
69892
(51K)
Saltburn
22 April 1957

Over the page you can see three photographs taken on Wednesday 4 September 1957 at West Hartlepool Station. The passenger train from Sunderland can be seen arriving from the north, standing at the platform and then leaving for Middlesbrough.

Class G5 67324
(51C)
West Hartlepool
4 September 1957

These are more views of West Hartlepool Station. The top photograph shows an engine at the south end as it leaves for Middlesbrough. Underneath, a train leaves for Newcastle from the north end

Class L1 67750
(51A)
West Hartlepool
November 1956

Class V3 67677
(51D)
West Hartlepool
September 1957

Overleaf, two aspects of Penshaw Station conclude the photographic record of journeys taken with the Runabout Ticket. A coal train trundles westward (above) while a passenger train leaves for Sunderland from the other platform (below). Like most stations on the routes of the Runabout Ticket, Penshaw is now closed and those stations that do survive no longer echo to the sound of steam trains.

Class Q6 63351 (51F), Penshaw, 6 September 1957

Class A8 69875 (51F), Penshaw, 6 September 1957

LOST ROUTES

The railway network was considerably larger in the 1950s than it is today and some of the most scenic routes open at that time are now lost to passengers. One such railway was the Border Counties line which linked the isolated villages of the North Tyne Valley with Hexham in the south and Riccarton Junction in the north. Here the morning train from Newcastle to Hawick via Riccarton Junction is seen crossing Hadrian's Wall near Chollerford in August 1956. Within two months of my taking this photograph (at great risk to life and limb) this line was closed. What was arguably the most beautiful railway in Northumberland was lost to travellers.

Class D49/1 62719 'Peebles-shire' (64B), near Chollerford, August 1956

Reedsmouth (Redesmouth) Junction was an isolated railway community in Northumberland, where the line from Morpeth (popularly known as the Wanney line) joined the Border Counties Railway. The photograph below was taken on the last day of passenger services – Saturday 13 October 1956. It shows the last 10.39am Saturdays-only train from Hexham to Kielder, decorated with a wreath on the smokebox door, passing the train from Riccarton Junction and Hawick.

Class V1 67639 (52C), Reedsmouth Junction, 13 October 1956

I took the photographs opposite at Kielder on the same day. It was a bleak lunchtime when the train arrived, which was appropriate for such a poignant occasion. The Hexham train was followed by an excursion train travelling from Newcastle to Hawick which is shown arriving at Kielder (top). Finally, the very last Saturdays-only afternoon train down the valley is seen preparing to leave Kielder Station.

*Class K1 62022
(52C)
Kielder
13 October 1956*

*Kielder Station
13 October 1956*

*Class V1 67639
(52C)
Kielder
13 October 1956*

The handbill reproduced overleaf advertises the excursion train to Hawick on the last day of services on the Border Counties line. Riccarton was the junction between the Border Counties line and the former Waverley Route to Edinburgh. Hard though it is to imagine, at that time there were no roads leading to Riccarton Junction – all of the small railway community's needs were supplied by rail, including funeral services. Nowadays the area is wooded, and what remains of the village is only the former generator o T. 1494X (HD)

BRITISH RAILWAYS

CLOSING OF NORTH TYNE BRANCH
EXCURSION TO
RICCARTON JUNCTION
AND HAWICK
SATURDAY 13th OCTOBER

Second Class Return Fares.

OUTWARD		Riccarton Jct.	Hawick.	RETURN	
	a.m.	s. d.	s. d.		p.m.
†SUNDERLAND ...dep	10 33	11/0	12/6	HAWICK..........dep	4 32
†South Shields .... „	10 22	10/9	11/6	RICCARTON JCT. „	5 5
†Tyne Dock .... „	10 27	10/6	11/6	Saughtree.............arr	5 10
†Monkseaton .... „	10 29	10/6	11/9	Deadwater .... „	5 17
†Whitley Bay .... „	10 31	10/6	11/9	Kielder Forest ...... „	5 22
†Tynemouth .... „	10 36	10/6	11/9	Lewiefield Halt ... „	5 27
†North Shields .... „	10 39	10/3	11/9	Plashetts .... „	5 31
NEWCASTLE .... „	11 10	10/0	10/9	Falstone .... „	5 40
Scotswood .... „	11 16	8/3	10/9	Thorneyburn .... „	5 47
Blaydon.................. „	11 20	8/0	10/0	Tarset .... „	5 51
Wylam .... „	11 28	7/9	10/0	Bellingham .... „	5 58
Prudhoe .... „	11 34	7/9	9/6	Reedsmouth .... „	6 2
Stocksfield .... „	11 40	7/6	9/0	Wark .... „	6 13
Riding Mill .... „	11 45	7/3	8/6	Barrasford .... „	6 20
Corbridge .... „	11 51	7/3	8/3	Chollerton .... „	6 24
	p.m.			Humshaugh............. „	6 28
Hexham .... „	12 6	6/0	8/0	Hexham .... „	6 41
Humshaugh............. „	12 20	5/6	7/3	Corbridge .... „	7 16
Chollerton .... „	12 24	5/0	7/3	Riding Mill .... „	7 21
Barrasford .... „	12 28	5/0	7/0	Stocksfield .... „	7 26
Wark .... „	12 36	5/0	6/6	Prudhoe .... „	7 32
Reedsmouth .... „	12 48	3/9	5/6	Wylam .... „	7 37
Bellingham .... „	12 53	3/9	5/6	Blaydon.................. „	7 45
Tarset .... „	1 0	3/6	5/6	Scotswood .... „	7 50
Thorneyburn .... „	1 4	3/6	4/9	NEWCASTLE .... „	8 2
Falstone .... „	1 13	2/6	4/9	North Shields .... „	8 37
Plashetts .... „	1 23	1/9	3/9	Tynemouth .... „	8 40
Lewiefield Halt ...... „	1 28	1/9	3/6	Whitley Bay .... „	8 45
Kielder Forest ...... „	1 35	1/6	3/6	Monkseaton .... „	8 47
Deadwater .... „	1 41	1/0	3/3	Tyne Dock .... „	8 56
Saughtree............... „	1 48	1/0	2/3	South Shields .... „	9 1
	p.m.		p.m.	SUNDERLAND .... „	9 16
Arrival Times	1 53		2 22		

†—Change at NEWCASTLE in each direction.

PASSENGERS ARE REQUESTED TO BOOK THEIR TICKETS IN ADVANCE.

PASSENGERS RETURN SAME DAY AS OUTWARD JOURNEY AND BY THE SERVICE SPECIFIED ABOVE ONLY

Children under three years of age, free ; three years and under 14 years, half-fares.

Further information will be supplied on application to the stations, agencies, or to S. Cott, District Passenger Manager, British Railways—Newcastle, Tel. 2-0741.

CONDITIONS OF ISSUE

These tickets are issued subject to the British Transport Commission's published Regulations and Conditions applicable to British Railways exhibited at their Stations or obtainable free of charge at station booking offices. Luggage allowances are as set out in the conditions.

Published by British Railways (N.E. Region)—10/56 Printed in Great Britain. T.P.W. Ltd. N/cle. B37½

shed, which houses a small museum. Even today the last 2½m of the road journey is along forestry plantation tracks. The photographs opposite, taken from the window of the excursion train, show the train for Carlisle waiting to depart and, watched by members of the Redhill Gang, the excursion train is leaving, assisted by a banking engine at the rear.

Class A3 60068 'Sir Visto' (68E), Riccarton, 13 October 1956

Leaving Riccarton, 13 October 1956

These images are of the busy scene at the border town of Hawick on that last day of services from Newcastle. An engine arrives at the depot, while the train from Carlisle to Edinburgh waits at the station. North British Railway locomotive 'Dugald Dalgetty' is preparing to leave the depot. These engines were known as 'Scotts' since they were named after characters in Sir Walter Scott's novels Nothing remains of the railway at Hawick; the area shown in these images has been developed into a sports centre.

BR Class 2 78047
(64G)
Hawick
13 October 1956

Class A3 60097
'Humorist'
(64B)
Hawick
13 October 1956

Class D30/2 62423
'Dugald Dalgetty' (64G)
Hawick
13 October 1956

The excursion train returned to Newcastle but a small group of enthusiasts alighted at Hexham to catch the very last service on the Border Counties Railway – the 9.15pm Saturdays-only train to Kielder. This was an occasion of great sadness. The train was decked with wreaths and people from the villages along the route turned up to say farewell to the railway. There were fireworks and, curiously, even people dressed up as ghosts along the way. The train arrived at Kielder Forest Station at 10.41pm, which marked the end of the official service, and normally the train would have returned to Hexham empty. However, special permission had been granted to the railway enthusiasts on this stirring occasion to return to Hexham with the train. This marked the official end of passenger services, although freight trains continued until 1963 and there was also the occasional excursion train.

Class V3 67651 (52B), Kielder, 13 October 1956

The high cost of repairs to the railway bridge across the River Tyne west of Hexham was the stated reason for the closure of the Border Counties Railway; had the line been more profitable, perhaps the necessary work might have been done and the line maintained.

Class J21s 65033 and 65110 (52B), Reedsmouth, 21 July 1957

Same engines at Deadwater, 21 July 1957

After 13 October 1956, freight trains and excursions used the line from Morpeth going west to Reedsmouth Junction in order to gain access. The photograph above was taken on a wet summer's day (21 July 1957); an excursion train arrives at Reedsmouth from Morpeth where the engines will run around the train and proceed, tender first, up the North Tyne valley to Hawick. Next, the train makes a stop at Deadwater Station on the Border, to allow ramblers to climb off. Note the rake of cattle trucks.

I was invited onto the footplate for the return journey from Hawick, and the photograph (left) shows the driver's view from 65033 near Shankend as the two engines tackled the climb to Whitrope Summit. These vintage engines had been designed at Gateshead in 1886 and were still providing useful service. Below, they stopped amid the wild moorland scenery of Plashetts Station (now flooded by Kielder Reservoir) to take on water.

Class J21s 65033 (52C) and 65103 (52C), Plashetts, 21 July 1957

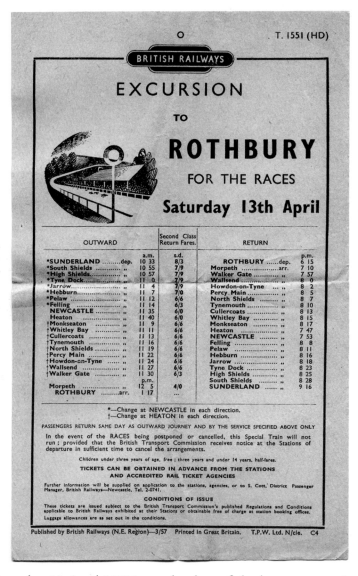

Saturday 13 April 1957 was the date of the last race meeting at Rothbury, in honour of which British Railways organised an excursion from Tyneside. The artist of the handbill draws a very grandiose picture of the course! Passenger services had

officially ended in 1952 so the excursion provided railway enthusiasts with a wonderful opportunity to travel the line. The photograph below shows the train at Scots Gap Station, now a retail outlet.

Class J21 65110 (52B), Scots Gap, 13 April 1957

Overleaf you can see the scene as the race-goers have arrived at Rothbury Station to be met by a lady ticket collector, which was most unusual. On p.165, at the west end of the station the engine moves onto the turntable next to a sadly deserted engine shed. The line finally closed in November 1963 and the site is now an industrial estate.

Class J21 65110 (52B), Rothbury, 13 April 1957

Class J21 65110 (52B), Rothbury, 13 April 1957

In 1957 it was possible to travel by train from Newcastle to Tweedmouth, then onwards down the scenic Tweed Valley line to St Boswells. By travelling through the border country on the Waverley Route to Hawick and Carlisle, you could return to Newcastle by the beautiful Tyne Valley line. On 28 June 1957 I set out on this circular journey. However, because the weather became atrocious near Riccarton Junction, I jumped trains at Steele Road and retraced my journey. In those days you could do such things with a privilege ticket!

Leaving Newcastle at 6.46am I arrived at Berwick at 8.12am in time to see the branch train from the fishing village of Eyemouth arrive. The photograph overleaf (top) shows the train preparing to depart from Berwick. The fireman is supplying the signalman with coal through the window, watched by two young girls.

Class J39/3 64843 (52D), Berwick, 28 June 1957

*Class J39/2 64917
(52D)
Coldstream
28 June 1957*

*Class J39/2 64917
(52D)
Tweedmouth
28 June 1957*

I returned to Tweedmouth to catch the 9.56am to St Boswells. At that time Tweedmouth had a grandiose main line station and also a locomotive depot housing nearly fifty engines. The train for St Boswells is shown at Tweedmouth (previous page, bottom). The photograph (middle left) shows the train at Coldstream on the return journey. Coldstream had been the junction of the mid Northumberland line to Alnwick, a line which was severed by flooding in 1948. Freight services continued to Wooler until 1965. The photograph below shows the return train at Kelso Station. Passenger services were withdrawn in 1964 and the line finally closed in 1968.

Class J39/2 64917 (52D), Kelso, 28 June 1957

St Boswells was on the North British Railway's main line between Carlisle and Edinburgh, which was known as the Waverley Route. Overleaf two young train-spotters can be seen, watching a stopping train from Hawick arrive as the station porter waits to load parcels onto the train.

The middle photograph below shows an express train from Edinburgh speeding through the station. St Boswells was also busy with freight traffic as the photographs on these pages show. This main line railway across the border was closed in 1969 and St Boswells, once an important junction, no longer has a railway.

Class B1 61354
(64A)
St Boswells
28 June 1957

Class A2/1 60510
'Robert the Bruce'
(64B)
St Boswells
28 June 1957

Class B1 61219 (68E), St Boswells, 28 June 1957

Class K3/2 61898
(68E)
St Boswells
28 June 1957

Class D49/1 62732
'Dumfries-shire'
(68E)
St Boswells
28 June 1957

Another very beautiful route lost to the railway traveller is the line from Middlesbrough down the North Yorkshire coast to Whitby and Scarborough. In the photograph overleaf (top) you can see the train for Whitby leaving Loftus on a wet April day in 1957. Below this, at Hinderwell, the signalman exchanges the token to enable the train to proceed down the single line railway to Whitby. A *token* was a safety measure, being a physical object, such as a key or a small disc, which the engine driver had to have in his possession before proceeding down a single track line.

BR Class 4 80119
(50G)
Loftus
23 April 1957

Class L1 67764
(51D)
Hinderwell
23 April 1957

BR Class 4 80117
(50G)
Sandsend
23 April 1957

In the photograph immediately above the evening train arrives at Sandsend to be greeted by a group of holiday makers returning to the camping coaches which can be seen on the left. Camping coaches were fitted out like caravans and provided supplementary income to many rural branch lines. On the next page (top) is a scene at Robin Hood's Bay Station.

BR Class 4 80117 (50G), Robin Hood's Bay, 23 April 1957

In the photograph overleaf the morning train to Whitby leaves the station at Fyling Hall for the picturesque station at Ravenscar, from where it is later seen leaving (this page, below) in a flurry of steam on 24 April 1957.

BR Class 4 80117 (50G), Ravenscar, 24 April 1957

BR Class 4 80117 (50G), Fyling Hall, 24 April 1957

AROUND BRITAIN

In those days, Inverness, Perth, Edinburgh, Glasgow, York, Shrewsbury, Bristol, Brighton, London and many other railway centres had youth hostels. Accommodation was provided to YHA members for a modest fee which enabled railway enthusiasts to use the hostels to explore the country. This chapter illustrates some of the journeys around Britain made by the Redhill Gang which were only possible because of the Youth Hostel Association.

Class B16/3 61463 (50A), York, 27 April 1957

In 1957 we made the YHA hostel at Clifton in York a base for an Easter holiday, to explore the railways of East Yorkshire. Many of these lines are now closed, such as the railway from York to Market Weighton which ran through the beautiful Yorkshire Wolds.

The rural nature of the line is captured in the next four pictures. The train from York to Hull via Market Weighton is seen approaching Stamford Bridge (top) and Fangfoss (middle). The image at the bottom of the page shows the train from Hull to York arriving at Londesborough.

Class D49/1
62723
'Nottinghamshire'
(53B)
Stamford Bridge
26 April 1957

Class D49/1
62723
'Nottinghamshire'
(53B)
Fangfoss
26 April 1957

Class D49/1
62717
'Banffshire'
(53B)
Londesborough
26 April 1957

The picture below shows a family full of anticipation as their holiday train, coming from York, pulls into the station at Market Weighton. At the bottom of the page you can see the Class D49 'Lincolnshire' at rest at Scarborough and overleaf in full steam leaving Filey. The line down the coast from Scarborough to Hull still exists but the trains are no longer hauled by steam engines.

Class D49/1 62724 'Bedfordshire' (53B), Market Weighton, 26 April 1957

Class D49/1 62710 'Lincolnshire' (53B) Scarborough 24 April 1957

Class D49/1 62710 'Lincolnshire' (53B), Filey, 24 April 1957

*Class D49/1
62717
'Banffshire'
(53B)
Flamborough
25 April 1957*

*Class D49/1
62701
'Derbyshire'
(53D)
Lowthorpe
26 April 1957*

176

The images on the previous page show the train from Scarborough to Hull entering delightful country stations at Flamborough and Lowthorpe. Even in those days there were very few passengers. Saturday 27 April 1957 was a busy day at Selby. This station was once on the east coast main line but now it has been bypassed. The push and pull service to Goole is preparing to depart (top). In the bottom picture you can see the porters guarding the pigeon baskets while members of the train crew stretch their legs.

Class G5 67250
(50C)
Selby
22 April 1957

LMS Class 4MT 43052 (50C), Selby, 27 April 1957

A few months later, in the summer holidays of 1957, the Redhill Gang toured Scotland and as usual we used youth hostels for accommodation. We spent the first two nights at the Edinburgh hostel from where we explored the railways of Fife. Then we went on to Perth and up the old Highland main line to Inverness, via Boat of Garten (opposite top) and Forres.

Class D34 62484 (63A), Perth, July 1957

Inverness Station (opposite middle) was triangular in plan, with lines for the north of Scotland and the Kyle of Lochalsh on the west coast. Following a night at the hostel we visited the shed and locomotive works of the former Highland Railway. Then we went on through Elgin to Keith (opposite bottom), Inverurie and Aberdeen. The scene at Keith shed (overleaf) shows the vintage engine of the Great North of Scotland Railway, 'Gordon Highlander', which these days is preserved and on show at Glasgow Transport Museum. After staying at the hostel at Feughside on the Deeside branch, we returned to Aberdeen to catch the train to Glasgow.

*LMS Class 5
45474
(63A)
Boat of Garten
July 1957*

*LMS Class 5
45474
(63A)
Forres
July 1957*

*Class J36
65304
(61C)
Keith
July 1957*

Class D40 62277 'Gordon Highlander' (61C), Keith, July 1957

Class C16 67501 (61C), Aberdeen, July 1957

Above you can see the pilot at Aberdeen Station busy with a mail train as the gang's exhausted train-spotters take a rest.

Glasgow youth hostel was our base for several nights as we tackled the sheds of this great railway city, undaunted by press reports of razor gangs roaming the suburbs. The city was world famous for its locomotive builders such as the Caledonian Railway Works at St Rollox, shown overleaf.

We did not return to Newcastle by the direct route through Edinburgh but via Ayr, Stranraer, Dumfries and Carlisle. This completed our summer expedition for 1957.

Caledonian 'Pug' 56025, St Rollox, July 1957

We made other expeditions in later years to Devon and Cornwall, Wales and the south coast – all made possible because of the Youth Hostels Association. Train-spotting was an absorbing pastime, and one which inspired many teenagers – like the members of the Redhill Gang – to explore distant parts of their home country at the same time as enjoying rail travel. This book has attempted to illustrate some of the fascinating scenic journeys which were possible fifty years ago such as the run through the Welsh mountains from Bala to Blaenau Festiniog, seen below.

GWR Pannier Tank 7409 (84J), Trawsfynydd, August 1958

The book has also tried to illustrate the railways of the mid 1950s when the steam locomotive was the principal source of power. I am hoping that it will have become obvious why trains and train-spotting was so attractive to teenagers of the period. Although the focus of this very personal book has been the Redhill Gang from the east end of Newcastle, their counterparts could be found throughout the country because train-spotting really was a national obsession. It easy to deride this hobby as simply 'collecting numbers' and – to be frank – for some lads it *was* no more than that. But there were many of us who developed an academic interest in the history and the technology of the railway. Some secured employment with British

BR Standard Class 4MT tank engine 80114 (61A), Deeside, July 1957

Class B1 61241 'Viscount Ridley' (52D), Fife, 1957

Railways, others became the backbone of the preservation movement which has been responsible for the restoration of dozens of steam locomotives and abandoned branch lines. There were always a large number who simply enjoyed the majestic beauty of watching a steam locomotive in action: to stand and stare at the 'Flying Scotsman' thundering past was, for us, to be in heaven. Back in 1957, none of us realised that steam locomotives would disappear from the public railway system within the decade, or that by now we would be looking back wistfully upon that time as 'a golden age of steam'. I hope that this book will serve as an affectionate reminder of a youth spent train-spotting and of that lost age ... *sic transit gloria mundi.*

INDEX OF PLACES NAMED IN PHOTOGRAPHS